HOLD YOUR

HOLD YOUR FIRE

Poems by members of Poetry ID

THE NORTH HERTS STANZA OF THE POETRY SOCIETY

poetryid.wordpress.com

2024

Published in Great Britain in 2024 by Poetry ID
The Settlement, Nevells Road, Letchworth SG6 4UB

All the poems in this anthology are copyright their respective authors

ISBN 9781739362218

Typeset by www.szcz.uk

Printed and bound by 4edge Limited, UK

CONTENTS

Foreword	1
About Poetry ID	3

ADRIAN BODDY

Scattering	5
Sonata	6
Winter Duo (night and day)	8

BARBARA WHEELER

End Game	10
Crucifixion II	11
Crucifixion I	11
Roxton	13
Stationery	15

PAUL GREEN

Archiving	16
Flight Path	17
Exclusion Zone	18
Machine: Q1	19

LISA MARIE CHAPMAN

Anxiety	20
Where are you?	21
Clophill Centre Woods	22

J. JOHNSON SMITH

Annie Kenney (13 Sept 1879 – 9 July 1953)	23
In the Body	25
Corpus	26
Reflections for the 27th January	27

DANNY LOMAS

Broken	28

ALAN DOGGETT

The School Reunion	29
The Month of June	30

TIM TAYLOR

I walked across a line 31
War Walk 32
Ariadne 33
The Ammonite 34

STUART HADEN

My Phoney Alphabet 35
Hitchin 36
Sim Me Try Me 37
a work of art 38
A Bridge Too Far 39

BARRIE KEMP

The Library 40
An Astronomical Black Hole 42
Books 44
The Cage 45

DAVID BIRKETT

Whose Name was Writ in Water 47
Prayer 48
A Phrasebook and Grammar
For Visitors to Gaza 49
The Love Song of a Dalek 50
'Like a nightingale with toothache' 51

ANNE TILBY

AI Guy 52

ALASTAIR McCALLION

Ambition 55
Museum, Cambridge 56
Shared Refuge 57
Luna 58
Apocalypse 58

JONATHAN WONHAM

Over the Top 59
Against War 60
Flour Massacre 61

Hind Rajab, 6 62
Real Time Genocide 63
A Glass of Water 64
Transformation 65
Sensitive Content 66

DENNIS TOMLINSON
Down in Kingston 67
Over the Hill 68
Tip 69
Home 70

MARK RANDLES
Ghost of a Gypsy Girl 71
Town 72
Fever 73
The Sea and the Sand 74
My Mother (Approximately) 75

NATHAN ADAMS
A Return to Romanticism 76
Felled Limbs of Trees 77
Olivia's Sonnet 78

YUKO MINAMIKAWA ADAMS
Cupid 79
Bangladesh 80
Egg 82

DAVID VAN-CAUTER
Hold Your Fire 84
The Rules 85
The Poetry of Climbing 86
Stop 88

ROSE SALIBA
Courage Wanting 89
Take It Easy 90
The Gift of Hope 91
Life Choices 92

JANETTE SIBLEY
2020, Operation, Work and Bang – Shutdown   93
Neither Here Nor There   95
Calming in Age   96
Teddy on My Breakfast Tray   97

SIMON COCKLE
The Three Magnets   98
January   99
Thunderstorm Cento   100

SHEENA CHAPMAN
As the rain pours through winter   101
The Irish Within   102
Corruption   103
The Sounds that Feed my Soul   104

Biographical notes   105

Acknowledgements   109

FOREWORD

Welcome to the twelfth annual collection of work by members of PoetryID, a collection of poems by 23 people associated with the group, which is the North Hertfordshire 'stanza' of The Poetry Society. I am pleased to report that there has again been an influx of new contributors, to both this collection and to the fortnightly workshop meetings at The Settlement in Letchworth. Fresh voices and fresh company keep the group alive. Our Zoom meetings are not running at present, but we are always looking for new ways to gather, meet and chat about poetry and everything else.

You will find, between the covers of *Hold Your Fire*, poems that wear a variety of different clothes – rhyme, metre, highly-charged prose, and more. The range includes a villanelle, rhyming couplets, a cento (a poem composed entirely of lines from other texts), sonnets and several fascinating pieces of no specific breed.

The things the poems wish to discuss span, as usual, a wide range of subjects and preoccupations, from Gaza to trains to stationery, and the differing tones and voices of the poems make up a wonderful babble (or Babel) of sound and meaning. Each piece holds its fire of creativity up to an increasingly confusing and challenging world.

We are continuing to work with The Letchworth Festival – via the irrepressible Hilary Kemp – David's Bookshop, and other local partners, on launches and events. We have also started taking stalls at a small number of literary fairs, both locally and in London. In 2023 we marked National Poetry Day UK with an open mic event at Hitchin Library, which attracted a good audience and some exciting new writers to the stage; we plan to continue this event annually. Please watch our website for news of events and other matters: https://poetryid.wordpress.com.

I hope you enjoy *Hold Your Fire* and are inspired by it to write, read and think about poetry, or to continue doing so.

Before you go in, here are a few quotes about poetry.

'Poets are the unacknowledged legislators of the world'
PERCY BYSSHE SHELLEY

'Poetry makes nothing happen'
W. H. AUDEN

'Poetry is the language in which man explores his own amazement'
A. E. HOUSMAN

'Poetry is language in top gear'
THE HEAD OF ENGLISH AT MY SECONDARY SCHOOL

David Birkett

ABOUT POETRY ID

Poetry ID is the Poetry Society's Stanza, or regional group, for North Hertfordshire, and we meet on Thursday evenings in term time from 7.30 to 10.00 pm at The Settlement in Nevells Road, Letchworth SG6 4UB. Here we hold regular workshops centred on various themes, after which there is an opportunity to read and discuss any work done. A number of the poems in this anthology started life as workshop drafts.

In recent years, we have taken part in many local events, including the Letchworth and Hitchin Festivals, the George Orwell Festival, the re-dedication of the Howard Park Gardens, and the Letchworth Garden City Heritage Foundation Fire and Fright Festival, as well as celebrating National Libraries Day and National Poetry Day.

We have brought poets of international reputation to read locally, including John Greening, Stuart Henson, John Mole, Helen Ivory, Martin Figura, George Szirtes, Jackie Kay and Penelope Shuttle, and we organise readings of our own, in Letchworth, at David's Bookshop, and in Hitchin, at The Highlander.

We are a friendly, outgoing and dynamic group of people and welcome new members. You can find out more by:

- visiting us online at poetryid.wordpress.com
- visiting us on Facebook
- or phoning David Smith on 01462 631285

You can also find us through the Poetry Society's website:
www.poetrysociety.org.uk/content/membership/stanzas/herts

ADRIAN BODDY

Scattering

The priest cadaver
asperges us
scourging the pallbearing sons.

The daughters
vying in black and veil,
perch on the steps,
rooked and ruthful.

The cousins,
platitudinous and plenty,
sing from frosted grief.

Lost children
creep past pillars
into the stony garden.

A dark hole,
a huge moon
and memory
unhome them.

The milk-teaed bone man is not missed;
enthroned in the dark
he reads Eumenides.

The leading lady
lies cold.

Sonata

1 He turns himself into a knife

He turns himself into a knife
and slices the moon;
but runs out of moon.

He slices up shadows,
but runs out of shadows.

He slices up love,
but runs out of love

He starts to slash up death
but death never runs out.

Enfeebled, he craves a last victim
and slices up the doctor with needles.

2 Of lemon trees

Your skin smells of lemon trees,
of orange blossom.

The men on the dockside stare
as if to slice you up.

The men in the hostel stare
as if to own you.

The boys on the street stare
as if to kiss you.

I hardly dare look.
I would never destroy or own you,
but what sweet bliss,
a kiss.

3 One less

One less station on the line,
one tree felled in the park,
one shop closed on the street,
one horse rustled at night,
one promise made.

One knife sharpened,
one curfew imposed,
one bullet in a door,
one brother disgraced.

One bomb on the church,
one meal uneaten
one priest decapitated.

One lover exiled,
one last kiss denied.

4 The moon is a knife

The moon is a knife
slicing the dark streets
into shadows,
where poets lounge.

The stars are bullets
piercing the student's book
at the upstairs window.

The clouds are poison
drifting into the lungs of paupers.

The snow washes clean
the tainted air of the city bank.

The sun pokes in its colonial gaze,
betraying us all.

Winter Duo (*night and day*)

1

The winter moon
casts its coldly stare
onto the birth of a romance.

The boy points up
offering the moon,
the whole sky.

The girl beholds
the shining
in his ardent eyes.

She nestles close
as if to say
I am here too.

2

She lies prone in the snow,
snow on her eyelids,
on her lips.

He stands by her
head turned aside
hearing nothing,

The field is white,
the sky is white

Neither hedge, house nor horse
interrupt;
nor intercede.

She lies prone in the snow.

He stands beside her
knowing nothing.

BARBARA WHEELER

End Game

You look up from the Monopoly board and whisper hoarsely
'You know I don't love you any more, don't you?'
I pack my overnight bag
and finger my ticket to King's Cross
and step out
with no means to travel on
as you have bought all the stations.
Outmanoeuvred
I shall blow on the dice
and leave it all to chance.

Crucifixion I

The mother of a child massacred by Herod watches the crucifixion

Some thirty-one years I bore my grief,
comforted that my son's death
was part of a greater plan. He was
torn from my arms,
a decoy for God Himself.
Some God He turned out to be,
bleeding and weak, and
crying out for shame.
They are saying that He died for us,
I say my son died for Him.

Crucifixion II

An imagined reply from the cross

Mother,
look up.
The thorns glisten
and my blood, diluted
by tears
streaks the face you hate
and my racked body.
I understand.
And yet, I do not.
There is a purpose.
I would say 'Trust me,
trust Him',
But now

this is too hard
for you, my friends,
perhaps for me just now.
Betrayed, whipped,
bound, a criminal,
shamed and crying out,
cruel nails tearing
wrists and feet,
where is the glory?
Where is the redeemer?
Do not look for me here
but come later
when I am finished
and you will find me
away from the baying crowds,
the bitter disappointment,
in a garden
raised gently by the Father
destroying death
which you have cursed so long.
Perhaps you will forgive me then?
Perhaps not;
but your son awaits you
and your joy will be great.

Roxton

7 o'clock
and it's stifling already in the caravan.
We push open the narrow door
and are met
with a barrage of heat.
We hear steam, gentle as yet,
hissing and whistling from the feathering valves
of workaday rollers and flashy showmen's engines,
Ruby, Sapphire, Victoria, George,
blue, red, green in line,
bound with straps and pipes of polished brass.
The men clamber over the engines,
oil cans and shovels
clatter and scrape as they tinker.
'Oy Steve, you've missed a bit!'
An oily rag meets its mark.
'Watch it, you...'
We women set to
with rags and Brasso
till everything that should shine does,
our gossip punctuated with explosions of laughter.
'She didn't!'
'She damn well did!'
Suddenly across the site
the mighty Gavioli launches into
'The Light Cavalry Overture',
faster than you've ever heard it played before,
with pounding chords and limpid arpeggios,
dazzling harmony and synchronicity.
A young girl appears with welcome mugs of tea.
We put down our rags

and take a moment
to survey the site, engines, marquees,
the sleeping fairground
that bind our world
and keep the children safe.

Stationery

Paper clips, trombones in French,
laze intertwined on the wooden bench,
how do they do that? I don't know,
they were uncoupled a week ago.
My Parker pen in its cardboard case,
blue, black and red inks, I can face
all correspondence with some pleasure
wielding this most valued treasure.
Two dead biros, green and black,
a plump one with four colours, back
when a teacher, I would fill
marksheets, coloured for each skill.
Two plastic rulers, a protractor,
compasses, a calculator,
a very good one indeed,
with functions I would never need
(I tried to give it to my grandsons
but they requested rather better ones).
Treasury tags and drawing pins,
used cartridges, assorted tins
with chalk, Blu-tak, a ball of string,
old coins, somebody's wedding ring,
erasers, or rubbers as we used to say
before America ruled the day.
hole reinforcers, three hole punches,
a photo of our girl in bunches
(she'd be embarrassed, she wouldn't like it,
so please pretend I didn't write it).
Pencils long, medium and short,
a pencil sharpener, various sorts of
paper, lined, A5, A4,
cards from friends who are no more.
Gollum, you can keep your ring,
stationery's my 'precioussss thing'.

PAUL GREEN

Archiving

A nation in slow motion. Xmas tree on the upper floor of the crumbling Edwardian mansion opposite flashes a distress signal. Time to mount the exercise bike and watch French TV detectives track a gang selling Semtex. End of tonight's bulletin.

I am exhausting my younger possibilities. This boy could have done good. Now he's a gong shimmering with nonsense songs. Filmic carriages slide past in back projection, clicking off the years, all that ticking off. I was dragging myself up to please everyone.

The continuity continues. Blue lights go out to receive the deceased. They are listed as ones and zeros, a data fest. All of us were so coded. We were good digits. I was a thought engine. You were binary and I'm such an iteration.

I'm breaking up my signal, my old face is fully booked. You're popping up face down. I was kneading your brain for tendrils of green electrons. On the frontline of sleep your faces lurk despite constant disintegration, all bulbous then ripped to floaty shreds, so much memory foams under my cold third eye and I don't have a template for it, my brain eats me alive.

I'm closing. There's a great noise of swarming. It's finally bringing erasure. Hold tight to your souvenir statues of Nietzsche, Voltaire, Newton. I'm going down slow with the Island. I'm closed.

Flight Path

Every hour on the hour
the refugees
fleeing their broken villages
clusters of unexploded bomblets
their burnt-out granaries
the rising tide of hot metal
bobbing on the boiling waves

we can't fit them into reception
the barges are leaking oil,
our bloody choppers won't reach air speed
too many aliens clinging to the undercarriage
and we are working so hard in our homes
to process the hot bodies

✳

Eight billion customers
eat the earth
smoke that old dino juice
and when it's gone it's gone
all brown
our empire of anthills
no gestaltbunker will keep them out
those hunger gamers

✳

No refuge in your headpiece
hiding with the dancing cyber-girls
the ghost dancers of Kabul, Fallujah, Homs, Khan Yunis
march through their blazing waiting rooms
towards our checkpoints

Exclusion Zone

Listen, Calliope, Miles Davis is playing
icy and muted tonight in his green shirt

so hold him tight like that
deep frozen in time

keep out the poets, all their viral words
beeping distress signals

the poets rampaging through the clubs
turning everything plural and louder

the poets are breaking like bad news
doing the Amen Break on their pointy heads

for the poets dance to rogue algorithms
they won't kiss the logo on your pedestal

Calliope they have one thing on their brain stems
an illuminated map of your underwear

Machine: Q1

Drivers called them 'Frankensteins'
brutalist, slab-sided, bleak boxes of steam

Engineer Bulleid subtracted all niceties
for his austerity weapon, no curving contours

but ramped up the pressures and the power
to pump heavy six-coupled iron

night after night after night after night
into blitzkrieg and low-flying bombs

glowing skyscapes of smoke
hauling milk trains, half-tracks, shells

and crowded corridors of squaddies
destined for 'somewhere on the South Coast'.

LISA MARIE CHAPMAN

Anxiety

It's like drowning but getting just enough air to keep surviving.
Traumas and fears keep me from thriving.
It's like a dark cloud or a shadow following behind me.
Feeding from me, I cannot deny it.
It's heavy and dark like a weight on your chest.
Unable to sleep.
Just and awake and a mess.
When will this hell end.
If they can't see it, they don't believe it.
But it's there.
Suffocating me in silence.
In moments of calm, it creeps in with dread.
At night I can't sleep, catastrophising in my head.
I have tried meditation and running and more.
Internally screaming.
But I look fine to the world.

Where are you?

All my life, I've looked for you.
Through the tall grass and through the woods
That longing to feel safe and understood,
I climbed mountains and travelled.
The stories I have collected.
In my pursuit to feeling accepted
Years of searching, feeling lost
Anxiety and depression were the cost.
It took some lessons and time to see.
The person I've been searching for
Was me.

Clophill Centre Woods

I've found heaven.
Its somewhere between where the grass grows long.
And I am completely alone.
The birds are singing, and the trees surround me
Like walls in a home.
The deepest breath fills my lungs,
But I do not feel alone,
I have the sunrays through the trees and the soft spongy grass beneath me.
I feel safe and content.
Like growing roots into the ground
Writing poems on parchment, no one's around.
At one with nature and feeling connected,
Like I could grow moss up my arms or blossom into the most beautiful flower
Or am I a weed?
A wildflower spreading its seeds.
Creating a meadow wherever it goes
What am I? I'm not sure I know.

J. JOHNSON SMITH

Annie Kenney (13 Sept 1879 – 9 July 1953)

So much to say about the Springhead mill-town girl
Grown up across the turn of the century
Working from the age of ten, then, age twenty-six, in 1905
one of a crowd hearing Christabel and Billington's[*]
inspiring talk that women should get the vote.

Entranced by the speakers
the thrill of a fight for social freedom
emancipation considered a right
by the dauntless women at the front of the stage
she joined them in voice and body, entered the fight.

Annie Kenney, now fearless activist, mill-town speaker
became an icon for the factory women
and a central part of the Suffragettes.
Having many brief liaisons with like-minded souls
ignoring the stations of breeding and class.

A founder of the WSPU,[†] harassing Parliament
breaking the laws and raising banners
that frustrated the norm, wherever she went.
Receiving prison, force-feeding and hate
with a passion that tempered her steel.

She carried the banner right up to the line:
imprisoned, enduring the 'Cat and Mouse Act'
part winning the cause in 1918
with older women getting the vote
but failing to help Christabel win a seat in the 'House'.

Annie Kenney, her course mostly run
settled and married, birthing a son

and where did she settle, now almost forgotten?
In Letchworth, Garden City, and died in Hitchin
but remembered in Saddleworth, with a statue in Bolton.
Annie Kenney, the emboldened Suffragette.

* *Christabel Pankhurst & Theresa Billington*
† *Women's Social & Political Union (WSPU)*

In the Body

Do you see my eyes?
In the mirror you stare blindly back at me
Unknowing,
But we have met.
I have carried you, unwavering, through the years
And you have denied me.
 When I sit on a chair
Leaning into that weary posture,
You place your hands on my knees
Supporting the weight of my tired body
Each hand a relic of the past,
Offering a heady vacuum, recalling a silence you once held.

But we have met,
In the street, just rounding a corner,
A shadow left behind to trip me up.
 Who are you soliciting and sniping along the way?
Your voice, a soft coo-coo taken over by a peacock scream
To an empty space.
 While in the window, looking down with racing mind
you calmly watch us walking past
And raise your hand a mite in silent admiration
As we string two steps, two words, along the kerb.

Corpus

A line or two, wrinkles laid flat
Sagged cheeks and mourning jaw dropped
Muscles, once firm, now loose flopped
All held close by a winding wrap.

Hair brushed; golden lashes on two closed petals
Resting. Pale cheeks forever frozen.
Nowhere can a prince be chosen
To kiss the beauty in still-fresh freckles.

Gone, lost to memory
A dream that insists it is alive.
A stiletto incubus to sink and slide
To crease the child that is part of me.
A line or two, wrinkles laid flat.

Reflections for the 27th January

Reflecting on the word 'holocaust'
I started writing a list
Of all those peoples
Killed for the sake of kin or caste.

From the Dawn of humankind
Survival was the plan, yet somehow
Power and politics have created,
while media related,
Genocide on an even greater scale.
Broadcast from the gates, the front lines,
The ditches and the fields,
The sight of ordinary people
Dying in extraordinary times.
The victim list is endless.
Religions or nations
Indigenous or clan
Aboriginal or Uyghurs
Gypsy, Inuit, Inca, Jew
Lakota, Sioux
Hindu and Sikh
Muslim and Christian
Tutsi, Hutu, or Bucha.
Holodomor and holocaust.

I will not go on, there are too many more.
Each corpse a testament in time
Of unbridled power
Man's inhumanity to man
A failure to learn.
Now's the turn of Palestine.

DANNY LOMAS

Broken

Shining on the outside with empty forced smiles,
Luckily they can't see the emptiness within,
Not depression, nor anxiety, the experience is of concern,
I walk and talk with a man-made mask to hide my true face.
I joke and play along with your conversation,
While nodding and visually listening,
I am simply somewhere else.
I've prayed and asked for answers with no apparent answer
Slaved, submitted and sacrificed my energy and time on the
ridiculousness of the race.
While this rat has chosen to no longer participate in your game,
He's gnawed and broken these chains.
Now he's on the outside looking at this mess,
How they control us and steal our hope,
We are all prisoners, no matter what steps we take,
The world is such a mess and hope is all but lost,
But relief lies true as it is them that can't see the truth,
The truth of how special we are and how strong we are together.

ALAN DOGGETT

The School Reunion

My school class were meeting in a pub
To have a few drinks and some grub
Some 40 years since I was at school
I didn't want to look a fool
So I entered the bar
And a voice from afar
Hello young Bill
Remember me I'm Jill
As we embraced and had a cuddle
My head was spinning I was in a muddle
But as I spoke to many more
The faces and memories came to the fore
Suddenly I could remember the past
And we laughed and chatted what a blast
Bill you fancied me said Kate
Do you recall our one and only date
Yes I replied but I found a new girl
We married and I am still with Shirl
What about the soccer team said Dick
We won the cup and you got a hat-trick
We remembered the teachers we had
And class mates who have passed away so sad
Oh said Derek remember Mr Fisher who we nicknamed Kipper
He would hit you with a slipper
Much to recall and share many a story
Yes those days were full of glory
But as we said our goodbyes
Some had tears in their eyes
The years were passing by
To meet again we must try

The Month of June

My favourite month is June
Our summer holiday will be soon
We have in sight
A day with the most hours of daylight
At dawn the birds come along
Such delight in full song
The sight of the full moon so merry
Known this month as the strawberry
Time to spend the hours
Appreciating the flowers
Get the garden looking at its best
To appreciate and take rest
For us dads a present and card may be heading our way
Because it's Father's Day
So where did the name June come from did you know?
The theory is the Roman goddess of marriage Juno
Much to achieve in many ways
Make the most of the thirty days
When the month is over it's very clear
We are halfway through the year

TIM TAYLOR

I walked across a line

I walked across a line.
I did not see it;
there was no sign or sound
when one foot or the other
first landed on the other side.
The earth did not look different
nor did the clouds change places
or the sun burn more or less
harshly than before.

An imaginary line, then?
a mere fiction on a map?
No. When I crossed,
that line sliced through my life
like wire through a cheese,
excised me from the web
of what I was. Before,
there was belonging
but not hope.

Here, I am Other,
an anomaly, a problem.
I have – I am – no one;
I own nothing but my shirt
and these sand-eroded shoes.
For all that, I am glad I crossed.
Better this dislocated
fragment of a life
than none.

War Walk

From lurid dreams, I wake to silence. Strange –
the air is still, no longer torn by screams.
Nor is it pierced by the stab of gunfire,
or shredded by the shock of bursting shells.

Despite my pain, my weariness, I rise
out of my ditch, drawn by this eerie sense
of peace to walk the battlefield, to see
what human madness wrought upon this land.

The earth is churned and pitted, acrid fog
is draped like cotton wool upon its wounds.
I do not recognize this place, its greens
replaced by brown and black, or livid red

and as I stumble through the drifting mist
I find the dead, some blown to pieces, some
incongruously peaceful, as in sleep.
I have no words for them, but as I pass

the quiet time is ending. Guns awake,
sharp cracks, bright flashes cutting through the fog
and soon enough the shells are falling. Yet
they seem unreal: why do I have the sense

that they can do no harm to me; indeed,
why do my feet not sink into the mud?
I have been walking in a circle – yes,
here is that ruined tree, the twisted wire
and there, in my familiar ditch, I see
a pile of corpses. One of them is me.

Ariadne

You will discover me
inside a maze of my own making;
a dream world, seeming real,
that obeys no logic, makes no sense.
I blunder from closed loops to
dead ends, unable to escape
yet barely knowing I am lost.

Others have attempted
to release me, but always found
the maze impenetrable,
its paths too densely intertwined.
Wary of monsters, they
avoided the dark corners, afraid
my prison might soon be theirs.

You are not the same. You have
the faith that somewhere within
these contorted corridors
there is someone worth rescuing.
You have the courage to come in
and the ball of thread
that will lead us out of here.

The Ammonite

It is a heavy thing; its surface, flat
and polished smooth, gleams with a glassy sheen.
An ornament, giving few signals that
this rock is not what it has always been.

Only the fragile walls encasing stone,
the perfect spiral structure, subtly show
the outline that was once a creature's home.
This object was alive, aeons ago.

It's beautiful, although the crystal grains
trapped in its many chambers give no clue
that what was here before had flesh, had brains.
Time has transformed it into something new.
A journey started in some ancient sea,
long dry, has come to rest – for now – with me.

STUART HADEN

My Phoney Alphabet

An *Alpha* male shouted '*Bravo!*'
Charlie was his name.
He *Delta* mean game.
His reputation was an *Echo*
of his *Foxtrot* fame.
He played *Golf* to train
and stayed in *Hotel India*
with *Juliet*, his flame.
A *Kilo* from *Lima*
bought *Mike* into frame.
Last *November* Oscar
called *Papa* in *Quebec*
and *Romeo* in *Sierra*.
Dancing a *Tango* in
Uniform made *Victor*
drink a lot of *Whiskey*
& get an *X-ray* of the
baggage the *Yankee*
was taking to *Zulu*,
a friend, whom he thought
he could depend,
if you believe *Alpha*,
bet & stick to the end.

Hitchin

A place to stop awhile.
No jaw dropping face.
You might smile
at this ancient place.

We traced a settlement
fifteen hundred years ago.
The Saxon Hicce's intent,
as rain broke chalk to flow,

to reside along the Hiz.
In time their to & fro,
to come, go & in a whiz
make hay from hamlet grow.

Sim Me Try Me

Am as sad as ever waiting for the goings and comings,
while the sautéed Donald Duck, BoJo 'n' Nic Bobbins,
Agents à l'orange at the top of Maslow's Pyramid,
look din on the world with Samson's strength as Gideon did.
Am passing this electronic phonic as Chinese whispers
along the Hawaiian Wei with the seven veiled sisters.
Are you sure my drift is as clear as the truth is hid?

We came from deepest, darkest Africa said Darwin.
'Via veritas vita' as naethin' was as sweet to him,
seein', meetin', blatherin' 'n' writin' a treatise.
And is that as useful now as when we thought of the birds 'n' bees?
Lovelock's work is better as it goes beyond what's here
Havin' bottled up so long we need to know what's where.
Am writin' this in hope it is better than chopping down trees.

a work of art

this poem is my attempt to describe the process from the start.
begin your observations with all your senses
& discover man's deceitful defences.
note & collect any anecdotal allegories,
fallacies & collateral familiarities.
comprehend the madness of humanity
& the mystery that is reality.
design with beauty, create with truth
& search for meaning in your proof.
record the inherent order of natural suitors
& include the past in imagined futures.
be aware of bureaucratic fences,
their polarities & contrived pretences.
nurture your curiosity & intuition,
use your discoveries & inspiration.
think with your heart, act mindfully from the start.
use unmanufactured natural matter,
plant your soulful seeds & scatter.
synthesise the factual with abstractions
create attention with distractions.
include your political philosophical belief.
show happiness in love, distress in grief.
balance convergent & divergent thinking.
recognise spontaneous reactions in a blinking.
perseverance creates successful resolution.
no doubt, all's inherent in human evolution.
the successful resolution of opposites creates a work of art.

A Bridge Too Far

Not for me the 'Stop talking', silent way
or the right hand, clockwise call to play.
Give me a party and a band any day.
Make music and understand
We are not here to follow some rule.
I am not some silly fool.

We want social intercourse and life
not dumb communication, trouble & strife.
We want fecundity, fruit & beauty
because life is meant to be enjoyed not a duty.

And by giving & creating
we are making & sustaining,
repairing& maintaining
this paradise as home.

We will not be others' play dough
to be sold, scold others & rolled as a dog bone
but flesh & blood with spiritual needs.
We are a small part of nature
living proactively as willow saps and bleeds.

BARRIE KEMP

The Library

The library stands proud
Somehow immune to demolition and development
Its doors – unlike its neighbours –
Are open to all bar none.

A Carnegie safe space
One pillar of democracy
A mixture of digital and print awaits all.

Its bookshelves stand like
The ribs of a stranded and dried-out whale.
These ribs are interspersed with readers and users
Of all shapes and sizes
Ages and origins.

Next to the children's fiction section
Are the pre-schoolers with their picture books and loud voices
Where eager young readers position themselves by the non-fiction in
pursuit of a challenge medal.

The adolescent readers huddle behind ribs zero to 399
Secretly reading about things
Their families would never tell them
Quietly ignoring their homework.

The adult readers are dispersed according to their needs:

Television-free readers are to be found within the fiction- Westerns,
Thrillers, Crime and Romance;
The business types are stationed at desks with desktops and laptops at ribs
400 to 799
All on the lookout for perfect deal or product;

From 800 through to 1000 is where
The amateur historians, research freaks, aspiring writers beaver away
In the hope of creating literature
That will lead to fame and fortune.

An Astronomical Black Hole

It started very quietly
Under the radar
So to speak.
An astronomical black hole
Came hurtling through space
Travelling billions of miles in a week.
It traversed the universe
The solar system
The Earth
And struck my life –
Just as I left for work.

Small things began to disappear
Such as socks from the wash
And expensive earrings worn by my wife
They had cost me a lot of dosh
And their loss had caused some strife.

All this talk about price rises and the 'cost of living'
Was it really caused by a black hole
Swallowing my hard-earned money
That kept disappearing
Never to reach my pocket
Despite 'net pay' being recorded on the wages docket?

And there's more:
I had parked the car at Heathrow
Carefully noting which park, column and row,

Only to return from holiday
To an empty space – what a blow!
The guy from security checked the CCTV
And advised that 'an astronomical black hole' had hit it
Taking to oblivion
The bodywork, engine and spare key.

My wife and I began to worry
About the children we had sent to Crewe
To stay at Nana's for R & R
Originally for a week
But she said 'Make it two!'

We rang their mobile phones
And got an answer
'We're in Sagittarius A Star –
Black hole at centre of universe – or was –
It wandered off its intended course!'

So now my wife and I
Having studied quantum physics and relativity
Are waiting for the day
When this black hole returns with our personal belongings
The socks, earrings, the car
And our most treasured relatives
Harry and Hermione.

Books

The sentinels of knowledge, of experience, and of the human condition
Stand cover-to-cover against the tide of screen distraction,
misinformation, and disinformation.
Five hundred years of the printed book
Bear testimony to their endurance.

Despite the Furies' claims of the Electronic Age
That books are obsolete a world now based on digital downloads and all
too brief interactions, books can survive and thrive in many parts of the
world.
To Kindle, Audible and Kobi!
Come back in 500 years and see who is still the Bibliographic King!
In the meantime
As physical book purchases increase as never before
The guardians of the public and private depositories
Still strive to make rational decisions
'To dispose or not to dispose; and what books shall we pass on?' (But
never in the process known as Fahrenheit 451!)

Physical books form one pillar of a civilised and democratic society
Alongside education, health and proper elections
Whilst one physical copy of Orwell's *Nineteen Eighty-Four* survives
No digital tyrant can ever claim
That the dystopia had had a happy ending.

The Cage

(On the 40th Anniversary of the Miners' Strike)

The ten colliers entered the lamp room
Each exchanging one of their numbered tokens for the corresponding lamp.
They walk towards the pit shaft where the cage is held taut by metal cable.

There's not much talk as each man gives a second token to the banksman.
It's a cold and breezy day, soon to be forgotten on the ten-hour shift.

The men are now aboard the cage with ten shovels, snap tins, and flasks.
The cage door is pulled across and bolted.
Suddenly, the giant wheel of the pit head
Spins as the cage
Plunges
Plunges
Plunges.

The square of light above
Is quickly replaced by ten lamp lights in pitch darkness,
Their beams dancing about like uncoordinated searchlights.

The men in the cage
Some young, some old, many middle-aged
Everyone with a personal history
With family waiting for them in the mining village 'Up top'.

The rising heat and humidity become almost unbearable.
Suddenly—
The cage jolts
And the ten lamps align themselves
As the cage door is unbolted and opened
And the men enter the horizontal shaft.

These men will shine a light for each other and watch each other's back today
Giving respect to King Coal
But on Saturday night at the Welfare
And on Sunday at Church or Chapel, they will give thanks for
another week of survival.

DAVID BIRKETT

Whose Name was Writ in Water

Thomas James Cobden Sanderson
A most atypical typographer,
Stands on a bridge in 1913.
He has resolved, on this Good Friday,
To sacrifice his typeface in Hammersmith.
Not the type itself, at first,
But the *matrices* and *punches* -
The hammers and the anvils
For movable type
That ensure each *glyph* is firmly set.

Firmly set, the signed commitment
(That his partner will inherit the typeface *Doves*
Should Thomas predecease him)
Jostles inside him, asserting, in anagrams,
That only the river should ever share
His lovingly nurtured creation.

Three years pass before this Thomas
Visits the Thames a Herculean
One hundred and seventy times,
Filling the water, like a liquid page
With all his letters and symbols;
An unpronounceable, terrible tract
Of jealousy and despair.

It was the *Doves*' last flight, until
In the twenty-first century, Robert Green,
A lover of fonts and of trawling the Thames,
Dredged from the mud one hundred and fifty
Fragments of wonder, and channelled them through
A digital stream of commands and instructions,

And the typeface *Doves* was born again, from water.

Prayer

Teach us to taste our daily bread;
To grasp it and declare it sweet.
We shall not look too far ahead.

We will not covet meat instead;
Should it appear, it will be meet.
Teach us to taste our daily bread.

If by tomorrow we are led
Then plant us firmly on our feet;
We shall not look too far ahead.

And when the moments which have fled
Say: *Feast on us and be replete*,
Teach us to taste our daily bread.

Our eyes have scales which can be shed,
And there is wonder near, to greet.
We shall not look too far ahead.

To what is here, let us be wed,
And not with phantoms lie, and cheat.
Teach us to taste our daily bread
We shall not look too far ahead.

A Phrasebook and Grammar
For Visitors to Gaza

March 2024

For *rescue* use *revenge*;
That town becomes *this rubble*;
Hospital turns to *hideout*;
Mercy won't translate.
Restraint declines regularly.
Be careful with your language –
Words may cause offence.

The Love Song of a Dalek

The landscape I will paint for you
Is a smouldering waste of ash and bone –
The annihilation of each love
That dared to be, before my own.

The scrapyard worlds of Rebus Four,
The Deep, where naught but night has shone,
Are lush, compared to my blighted heart
When all of my wavelengths signal you gone.

Come, glide with me, and witness that
Which rays and missiles cannot do –
The swift extermination of
The borders between me and you.

'Like a nightingale with toothache'
(*a musical instruction by Erik Satie*)

The nightingale with a toothache
Sings of an awkward, clumsy love
That does not fit – a hand in glove –
Into the moulds that stories make.

The phoenix with the broken wings
Stirs its ash in a failed ascent
Away from its environment;
The burning song is all it sings.

The unicorn comes limping, slow,
To kneel and bow; it asks no fee
Of unimpaired virginity;
It takes what humans can bestow.

Embrace this ark of creatures that
May not attain an Ararat.

ANNE TILBY

AI Guy

Hey Baby – that's me – Don DJ
shock jock, super-tanned, in control,
ensuring that you have your say –
entrepreneurial media mogul
your personal, ulterior motivator.

Keeping it real – that's my style.
I hear how my public feel,
I intend to be around a while,
millions envy my situation,
fans adore me, I'm their inspiration.

With influential 'friends' in far-flung places
All those big bosses – they my type – like
my mate Andrew Tate – believe the hype!
I was dining with Putin,
then after, thought – I'd nuke him …

You can't trust Russians
as far as you can throw them.
Whilst we're on the subject of guns –
We need more… more guns.
Let's ask KKK to join the play.

I identify with everyone… but not queers
or lesbians or dykes…
or Jews or blacks or whites
or Germans (they came from germs)
Mexicans go home!

The ANP all dote on me
and those little islands, in the sea...
they were never meant to be.
(*nor was that lil' Swedish girlie with pigtails*)
No such thing as Climate Change. Pah!

Ignore the crazy weather...
Floods, hurricanes ain't so strange
let's put it off for later.
God bless America.
You can cope with it together.

Take that Amazon Rain Forest – so vast, so bland...
What a mess! But hey –
Now *there's* Real Estate potential,
Like Sun City, another golf course, or a new Disneyland.
Naturally, nature looks after itself.

That wild stuff was never meant to last
(there's always a solution)
Our sewage and waste are pumped out fast
Green Wash to Pollution!
trash ain't a problem, we shoot it into space.

It's China cooking plastic –
there's no accounting for their taste.
China (*they're the Covid people*)
that segregated race.
In fact, don't buy anything from China... don't click

Some guys go through the door
But our guys...
Our guys go through the walls
They're good.
Make America great again

We build bigger better.
Expansion is the answer
My body is a temple
I hate ugly people. Don't you?
I need to be surrounded by *beautiful people*

And beautiful dogs
Those beautiful dogs (I eat only beef)
Those Afghans...
those *hysterical* women in Afghanistan –
whose side are they on?

Press the button? I can press all the buttons,
I *am* the zeitgeist –
my finger on the pulse,
ignore all the rumours,
most of them are false

Tactic: TikTok. What's not to like?
The future is bright, the future is orange.

ALASTAIR McCALLION

Ambition

'If I knew where poems come from, I would go there'
Michael Longley

The writer, much admired, has a poet's gaze –
Gentle, searing – and an ear
Acute, discerning, wisely open.

A badger, crossing his moonlit path,
Reminds him of the gait
Of a murdered big-arsed friend,
And the sound of whooper swans
Delights and sometimes disturbs him.

Admission of ambition
To hang on his trailed coat
Is heavy with a fear
Of kindly-smiled encouragement
For a lofty aspiration
That's more hope than expectation.

Museum, Cambridge

Saint Edmund of Abingdon stands beneath
The open-tread staircase that leads up to
The Library floor of Kettle's Yard. Catto's
Found figure – nature-sculpted willow branch
Felled and charred by a lightning strike, a spark
Of fire, an act of God – stands pot-bellied,
Meditative reminder of carvings
Of saints in medieval wayside shrines.

Sculptor-crafted and sunlight-reflecting,
His contrast is exhibited across
The Bridge to the old Cottages. Almost
Ungainly, caught in transition from one
Ballet movement to the next, the Dancer
Captures in bronze the exquisite stillness of motion.

Shared Refuge

(after Chimamanda Ngozi Adichie)

The news is like a vicious uprooting.
He was walking past my house, just last week;
Not sprightly as of yore though, I noticed –
He would have raised an eyebrow at 'of yore'.

He might pause to chat on rugby, books, birds,
Perhaps to set the world to rights, again.
He mused 'they'd' given him two years, but that
Was ages past – a relished pyrrhic victory.

No more chatty pauses, no rugby, books,
No birds. And, oh, how glib condolences
Can feel as we wrestle with our sadness
And try to find shared refuge in our grief.

Luna

She lies on her back, blushing slightly, like
A louche languid courtesan, denizen
Of belle époque salons; pale half moon
Awaiting her sun god, his gold hair streaming
As sunbeams exploding the patiently
Dawning horizon. He seizes her,
Casts her down to the subterranean
Darkness, below the farthest horizon
Into the darkling abyss, now consigned
To pull on her silver shoes starting again
To explore other darknesses until
She stands full-faced, brightly shining, serene
Queen of the Night over vanquished Apollo.

Apocalypse

wars are raging, and there are
rumours and more, more rumours of war;
glimpse a pale horse and await
the moon that turns to blood

JONATHAN WONHAM

*Over the Top**

Oh, you went over the top!
You went too far...
Beyond normal, expected, or reasonable limits.
You were excessive, outrageous.

Or is it over the top like: I thought
the decorations were way over the top.
Or, your gift to me was far too generous –
it was over the top!

Or, perhaps, was it like:
we're going over the top!
Meaning over the parapet, out of the trench,
like, you know, at the start of another futile attack.

---

* *After Israel had rained US-manufactured weapons on Gaza for four months, killing more than 30,000, President Joe Biden said on 8 February 2024 that Israel's response to 7 October 2023 was 'over the top'.*

Against War

What would it be,
a poem against war,
without anger?

A piece of fake
news, pretending
slander.

What would it be,
a poem against war,
without love?

A dropping, not
a throwing down
of the glove.

Flour Massacre

Their bullets left
no uncertain claims
in our bodies.

Meanwhile, we left
what we should not have left:
young lives, young blood.

Our minds said 'leave'
but our stomachs said 'stay'.

Forgive us our eagerness.
We took what we could.

Meanwhile,
they took our lives.

Our deaths are counted up,
teetering precise,
a little more every day.

Our eyes in here
are blurred through hunger.
Why are your eyes blurred
out there, in the world?

Hind Rajab, 6

These were her
belongings:
a pink backpack,
one sock
and a stapler.

Real Time Genocide

Do you have time
to watch the real time
genocide going on

between your TikTok
how to get firm buns
how to make a salad

how to safely return
the online purchase
that doesn't fit?

Genocide in real time
do you possibly
have time for it?

A Glass of Water

Reflections on a glass of water
at an old café table by the sea.
She peers through the mirror of the past
at the happy self she can no longer be.

She watches herself softly laugh
alone with the boy she loved –
the cool glass rising to her lips,
the boy's eyes warming her blood.

Gazing back through the one-way mirror
a tear comes to be wiped away.
Am I only made of tears now? she asks,
a glass that overflows with lost days?

Transformation

She has always been a kind of superwoman
cradling the faces of children, feeding them
out of a bottomless cauldron of love.
She has always been extraordinary even when
confined by four walls. Now she feels pain
and joy when the sheet flutters beside her head –
this extraordinary tent her husband made
telling her it's their cocoon of rebirth.

It comforts her, the children sleeping
curled together on some plastic sacks,
her husband patrolling, using telescopic eyes
to look for dropped handfuls of flour.
Her youngest, sleeping now, also shows signs
of developing amazing powers, calmness
like a piece of reinforced steel, her eyes
flashing sometimes in the dark when she wakes.

Sensitive Content

I can't click any more
on the blank, black screens
where is calmly written
'Sensitive content'.

I don't want to see any more
graphic or violent scenes
and I'd like Israel and USA
to stop making that for me.

DENNIS TOMLINSON

Down in Kingston

In the car park
leaves are flying.
I place the Blue
Badge on the dash.

Your wheelchair feels
heavy uphill.
A hard-hat man
gives us a smile.

By the wayside
charity shop
the usual
beggar's not there.

Inside, you're in
your snowflake top.
The waitress pours
sweet wine at last.

Over the Hill

Somewhere behind
rhododendrons
or in bare trees
birds are singing.

Over the hill
comes a big bus,
long ride to reach
the hospital.

They come and go
by the entrance –
Richard! We walk
bright corridors.

My wife's sleeping
with a light snore.
Behind the desk
a Christmas tree.

Tip

The car loaded:
bags of pillows,
a copper pipe,
a VCR.

Streets damp and cold.
By the food store
a few jackdaws
peck at stale bread.

A hi-vis man
gives me a smile,
waves me through. Crow
on a dustbin.

I swing the sacks
into the pit
with enjoyment.
Country music.

Home

Hanging baskets
flank the entrance.
A wet pigeon
pecks at the ground.

No-one's sitting
in my wife's chair.
A helper says
personal care.

They wheel her in,
clean but weary,
her fingernails
now painted pink.

She looks at me.
From the next chair
Mary enquires,
Do you love me?

MARK RANDLES

Ghost of a Gypsy Girl

I was seven when I walked with my mother to the river,
to paddle apprehensively in the stickleback stream.
With a cane-stick and a minnow net,
the sun shone on my jam jar,
as we walked my baby sister beside the bulrushes and reeds.

I wandered further onward and saw a line of low caravans
belonging to the travellers that were camped along the bank.
There I saw a gypsy girl,
wading toward me through the water,
where a lonely weeping willow tree bent its branches down and drank.

Then suddenly all hazel-haired, the girl she pounced upon me,
held her nails to my wrists as she demanded 'What's your name?'
A cloud passed across the sun
and I felt God get distracted;
I fell into the water, as tears stung my face.

Then the girl turned away and ran, to her father who was scolding,
while my mother fished me up and sat me soaking, on the ground.
I watched the gypsy girl glance back,
her hazel eyes all fearful.
Apart from my chided sobs there was no other sound.

*

Today I drive that river road, park my car along the gravel path,
weeping willows and bulrush reeds, rustle along the plain.
I hear the ghost of the gypsy girl,
calling me from her riverbed,
saying 'I never meant to haunt your life – I just wanted to know your name.'

Town

I loved this town.
Its edge by the by-pass,
and oxbowing brook.
Perimeter where tall pylons strode
above fields of cows and cowpats.
Where fighter jets flew in
aerospace factory skies.
Built by weapons systems workers.
Working three-shift, seven-day patterns;
globally warming the cold war to hot.

But now the bypass is a motorway,
and the brook built upon.
Pylons replaced
by a solar panel farm.
Sons of weapons systems workers
are stacking supermarket shelves.
Heads of multinationals
are pissing themselves.
The snowless globe is still warming,
and today's wars are already hot.

Fever

The fever caused me to lose you;
I couldn't fathom your form or your shape,
only a crumpled quilt for your body,
vacant pillow for your beautiful face.

As I sank into you, you vanished,
I fell to the mattress bereft.
Your legs not tangled in eiderdown;
your head not on the pillowcase.

So I lay there without you till morning
until dawn shone on my face,
I clutched at your shoulders that weren't there,
felt your memory getting erased.

I dozed and I drowsed until lunchtime,
slept still through the warm afternoon.
I awoke just as dusk was falling,
and gathered a search party for you.

Though the bed was so big, I knew you were there,
across the expanse of full memory foam.
I set off that night on my journey,
to find you and fetch you back home.

The Sea and the Sand

Once they were lovers,
the sea, and the sand,
inseparable as
ink in ink.
The sea
would serenade with
whisperings of shells.
He'd kiss the hem of
her shoreline; she'd skirt
the edge of his moonlight.
Both forever left silvered
with sprinkles
of stars.

My Mother (*Approximately*)

Walking in the wrong direction,
along Ware High Street;
eating a cardboard sandwich.
I stare at the wet pavement
in sadness and defeat.
The sky darkens from
purple to grey and
a fox scavenges the urban hedgerow.
My sister's face appears on the phone
to say that our mother is tired
of all three of her creations:
And our father
is not there to explain.

NATHAN ADAMS

A Return to Romanticism

Had you caught the way I did;
Tree-dappled sun break across her face
To fleck pied eyes with gold light till
The stillness was stolen by playful grin;

Had you beheld the heads of foxglove
Bow, and bate the breath of summer
Breeze – to confront her knuckles with
A kiss;

Or bore ears to hear the beauty
Of branches and the brook and bullfinches sing
To match in cadence and grace: her giggling;

You may, as I did, have lost your lungs –
Given them over to the verdure
And noted that every absent breath
Be not a thing you think to miss.

Felled Limbs of Trees

Felled limbs of trees decay in midst of mournful penstemon
Who loom with bowing heads; declaring kinship with rot
Gather like guides to usher the soul to soil.

Moss-encroached birch glower many-eyed against the procession,
Wailing their laments by way of amanuensis through the wind –
The reapers' petals shiver as breeze brings night in,
Where obsidian weeps its silver tears
And our lunar body returns ill light to illuminate with waxy veil
The corpse; its lichen-strewn rind set lambent.

Olivia's Sonnet

Legs tangled, breath upon her nape. In sleep
We dream of words lost unto waking hours
And nomenclators are, informing the
Impossible, the lexicon of love.
Its every idiom doth defy the
Grasp of the cognisant-mind governed tongue
But crawls out of slack throats in slumber; loves
Precise expression; failed somniloquence.

White horses fall off of gusts tempered and
In silver lulls drown. And snow's fatal crash
On the loch sounds the same soft utterance
As lovers joined in dreams of poetry;
That will leave an impression on the mind,
But fade and dance as a ghost on the tongue.

YUKO MINAMIKAWA ADAMS

Cupid

The day love was classified
as an endangered species
Cupid broke his bow and arrow.
After he stopped using his arms,
they gradually decayed
and came off in the end.
The only job he could do
was working as a model for an artist.

Being surrounded by apples and canvases
Cupid posed for a painter.
While the artist's eyes were tracing his contour
he was filled with the glow
he'd forgotten for a long time.
He touched the apples with his toes
and loaded the fruits with love.

The first day of exhibition
Cupid kicked out the apples from the painting
and shot the viewers randomly.

Bangladesh

for Rana Plaza in April 2013

We're stitching your future skins with a sewing machine.
We're piercing your future skins with a needle.
Your inborn skin should be covered with the skins we stitch.
You cannot go out and walk without the skins we stitch.
Your future skins are cotton, polyester, nylon, Lycra.
We often sew frills and gathers on your future skins.
We often sew buttons and zippers on your future skins.
The future skins of your arms, body, legs and thighs are all separate
until we join them.
While we're stitching your future skins from morning to dawn,
you're moulting the skins that we stitched up in the past.
You say you have pale blue skins and you also need green skins.
You say you only have warm skins so you need cool skins.
You say your children are growing up so quickly.
You think T-shirts are flying from the sky.
You moan your skins tend to be thinner these days.
You grumble your skins get easily flabby.
But you want to get your future skins as cheap as possible.
When your skins are torn, you're not to mend them.
You bring them to a waste site. You bring them to a charity shop.
You say you dispose of your skins to look to the future.
As we're stitching your future skins incessantly,
our eyes, hands, arms and shoulders are getting numb
and we feel our limbs falling apart.
We wish we could stitch up ourselves –
from fingers, shoulders, head, spine, hip to tiptoes,
even if a needle could perforate our flesh.
The building where we're stitching your future skins
is vibrating all the time,

shaken by sewing machines we're using for your future skins.
Some of us have found a crack on the wall
in the building where we're stitching your future skins.
We don't want to stitch your future skins until the wall is fixed
but it's more urgent for our boss to stitch your future skins
than to join the present crack.
We've decided to stitch your future skins again tomorrow
because catching up with your moulting
is the only way we can survive.

Egg

Please do not think
I was born
because I wanted to be born.
Please do not think
I pecked my shell
because it is broken.
This egg had been shattered
while I was still unsure
if I wanted to be born.
While my mother was away from the nest
someone shot it.
Before I was taught
what the world was like,
the light hit me.
Winds slapped me.
The eggs of my siblings,
incubated in the same nest,
were all shot dead.
I was the survivor.
I was the only one
who came into the world.
My mother told me
I was a child of miracle.

I'm not a child of miracle.
I'm not a child of joy.
I am a child of violence.
I was born
because of the failure
the sniper made.

Each time my mother showed
her delight in my birth
I doubted it.
When my beak caught a caterpillar
for the first time in my life
it didn't taste.

After my feathers grew
and I flew in the sky
for the first time in my life,
I swayed in the winds.
Whenever my mates
praised my singing
I thought it was a lie.
The force that made me be born
was the force trying to crush me.
Please do not praise me.
Please do not encourage me.
I was born
urged by the power
trying to destroy me.

DAVID VAN-CAUTER

Hold Your Fire

My students ask *Whose side are you on?*
like it's a bloody football match
and simply a matter of picking blue or red
and cheering from the crowd.

But bloodsports aren't my thing –
I am outside the stadium, pretending
that I cannot intervene
seeing the headlines hearing the screams

This is not my war but is it war
when one side wields a pocket knife the other – bombs
and the spoils – thousands of dead children?

Tell me, what is gained by this?
Hold your fire. For the love of god hold your fire.

The Rules

At first we threw our stones into the sea
like they were distance markers.
What are the rules? I said.
Who needs them? you replied
and kept on throwing.

Then, drifting into sight, a wicker skeleton,
its ragged framework now our target –
contact, stone to cage,
one point per hit.

The tide was coming in.
We saw it was a lobster pot,
cut loose, rotating, free.
As it turned, a hole revealed itself –
we aimed for that.

Closer, easier, till it rested there,
basket side up.
The challenge now: how close we could both get
without our feet touching the water,
our footsteps folding stones together,
trying not to fall.

I wish we could have stayed on that beach
like wayward lobster pots,
tossing these rules away.

The Poetry of Climbing

Rule 1:
Do not take on the mountain
unless you are prepared.
Start small – consider a tree
or a brick wall –
these are more relatable,
easier to quantify.
8000 metres – insurmountable.
10 or 20 – that's a breeze
and well within parameters.
If you cannot comprehend a brick, a leaf,
you should avoid the distant, foggy peaks
of intangible ambiguity.

Rule 2:
It is not a mountain – it's a metaphor.
Wordsworth didn't spin his rowing boat around
for a lump of rock.
It is alive and should be treated with
humility, respect and fear.
Do not hack away with your pick
and kick your spiked boots in – instead
caress and tease its secrets free
with gentle fingertips and whispering –
you might learn something.
Rock is softer than you think.

Rule 3:
Patience. It's a game you're destined to repeat
over and over, the path upwards refined
before its revelation.
A vertical cliff lacks all perspective,
you are in the hands of gravity
and time is meaningless.
Stop and breathe, take in the view,
appreciate the journey.

Rule 4:
This is not the poetry of falling –

do
not
fall

Stop

Suella spreads her xenophobic bile
from a podium, applauded by Farage,
where last year Truss, the great blue hope,
was bigging herself up, giving it large
with talk of mini-budgets that would save
the sinking ship of England, lost at sea,
waylaid by leftie lawyers, human rights…
How dare they? It's the stuff of anarchy.
No, let's have culture wars, so we distract
the masses from the real world, the one
where immigration is our history:
read a book – and look up 'Anglo-Saxon'.
The tide is turning on your swamp of blue:
it's not the boats we need to stop – it's you.

ROSE SALIBA

Corage Wanting

Sick to the stomach,

watching genocide on screen;

powerless to act.

Scared to speak out or object

in case the guns turn on us.

A Tanka poem – In the name of Humanity
(written as part of the Tanka Challenge – Without Love)

Take It Easy

Hold your fire
of wounding words,
they leave a scar
like a bloodied nose.

Take a slow deep breath
and count to ten
before you shout or shoot
that harmful gem.

'Is it kind?
Is it necessary?
Is the timing right?'

Will it keep the peace?
Or prolong the fight?

Compassion, forgiveness,
not always easy.
Release the breath
relax, be breezy.

Take your finger off the trigger
and lower the gun,
till the moment has passed
what can't be undone.

The Gift of Hope

Ho'oponopono,
Hawaiian blessing
of forgiveness:

'I am sorry
Please forgive me
Thank you
I love you'

Reconciling differences, conflicts and law.
Inner and outer, let's heal them all.

Letting go of stored anger, resentment, so raw.
Calming emotions, when you just want to roar.

Forgiving ex-lovers, siblings and more
so you can walk lightly out of the door.

Could it work on world leaders, hell-bent on war?
They cause so much suffering; homeless and poor.

Give hope.
Forgive.
Make love, not war.

Life Choices

It's love, not fear
that will change the world.

Kindness, compassion and joy.

It's care, not harm
that will heal our world.

Kindness, compassion with joy.

Competing and hating
are killing us all.

No kindness, compassion or joy.

The Earth needs love
not bombs from above.

Kindness, compassion and hope.

A spiritual path
could have the last laugh.

But by then, it might be too late.

Let's choose:
Kindness, compassion and joy.

JANETTE SIBLEY

2020, Operation, Work and Bang – Shutdown

The fathomless depths of depression
Reaching out, is it possible?
Voices, major voices, tiny voices, which is in command?
Why did they start, how did they start?

Wasn't I always there, was I too busy to share?
Shared ups and downs, some so good, some black.
Trying to mediate a bad relationship; was I listening?
Was I too busy to share?
Facing aggression, confrontation, trying to appease? Hello?

40 years old, 30 years of physical pain resolved,
I must be well and back on track?
The fathomless depths of depression
Voices, major voices, tiny voices, which is in command?

Mental anxiety, no work coming in
Walking, reading, television; having a drink.
Watching television, having a drink
Walking to Nisa, drinks on the settee; with the television

Were we watching, did we see, hear the signs?
Yes, we reacted, no more hiding, face reality.
Speak the truth, listen, recognise the illness.
Wait, time and peace, hugs, food and tea.
Time to face recovery and hope.

One Year No Beer, I tried before, 80 days plus.
Not an alcoholic, do it on my own.
Returned, listened, didn't share, Not an alcoholic!

32 days dry, drove by Nisa; stopped, Not an alcoholic!
5 days, lost the plot, comatosed on the settee.
They were watching, listening, family fill the breach
Agencies alert, speaking, sober up.

Applying for college, seeking a new career
Return One Year No Beer, listen, talk and Share.
I am unwell, I have a life-threatening allergy
I am an alcoholic and I want to Survive!

It won't be an easy ride, but people on my side
I must recognise my triggers, keep strong and positive.
I am unwell, I have a life-threatening allergy
I am an alcoholic and I want to Survive!

I am an alcoholic! I want to Survive.

I was the outsider looking in, trying to understand from their side, it's an
ongoing fight, but, the last temptation meant they reached out to me - a
first, I was so proud.

Neither Here Nor There

Neither here nor there
Neither here nor there
Neither coming nor going
Seeing but unseen
Seeking purpose
A need to belong,
A time to come forward
A part of a new society,
Not to be disseminated, ostracised,
Alienated by my home or transportation
I seek refuge!

Calming in Age

My retirement is full and busy, walking, crafts, singing.
I often wonder what others are missing
Loneliness as work finishes, no hobbies, is there joy?
Their joy must be what my brother calls
Rich women taking afternoon tea.
I must thank my father for his gifts of reading, writing and walking.
My mother for her love of embroidery and knitting.
Others drown in spirits and wine,
Or comatose in front of the magic lantern.
Life can be long; empty and sad,
Incredibly, tenacity may be the strongest driving force;
But taking a moment to review; going shopping,
Reading magazines and doing puzzles,
Taking coffee, meeting friends and interacting
Television before bed; maybe a shorter day.
Reminiscing, fun gone by with long anecdotal stories shared.
A healthier sleep is as good an answer
To life's shortening years.
Life's gift is not money or traditional learning,
It's seeing each day in beauty, despite one's ails.
Sharing in age, recognising our childhood is still within.
Realising status is the game and not the result.

Teddy on My Breakfast Tray

Every morning bear lies back, he is cosseted in his gingham-patterned
blue and white towel.

His belly depressed into the sink he looks out in a melancholy gesture,

bright-eyed with a shiny nose and whiskers

with his legs open, stretched up in the air, and his left arm luxuriously
extended along the towel.

He is in repose.

This bruin is only a little longer than the sink he fits, his plush fur, only
slightly worn, shimmers.

His pads are soft, moulded and shiny from thumb stroking.

One ear rests against the makeshift shelf, ready to unbalance the pretty
pink perfume bottles.

And the pink rose-hip patterned towel dragged out from the towel rail,
to warm his shoulders,

might just result in the blue-white porcelain falling down as well.

Every morning I look at the shining brass Victorian taps and wonder:

There is a pink bar of glycerine soap, turn on the taps, give Ted a wash?

No, that would mean disturbing the image of Teddy on my breakfast tray.

SIMON COCKLE

The Three Magnets
or 'The people – where will they go?'

Ebeneezer dreams of magnets, pulling folk
From town to country, then, from country, town
And thinks a new To-Morrow. Sitting down,
He jots a logo: lists of pros and cons
Of life in city slums but wages rising,
Chums to chat with. So, too, with village ways:
Fresh air, and meadow sunshine, in decay
With idle blight and boredom, jobs declining.
Solution? Take the best of both! Behold:
The New Town-Country, a pastoral/urban idyll,
A cipher of Well-being. In the middle,
A Central Park where New Utopians stroll.
Did he succeed? Is this the town he scribbled,
Or are we still caught between the magnets' pull?

January

night is an open grave
and the only respite is morning

when the sun files along
the edge of the earth

we know there are trees
unseen behind shadows

their branches catch your breath
and the leaves persist

but the ghost in the corner of your eye
is the beat of a wing long since past

your reflection in the eyes of a fox
disappearing with a whisper

not enough light
not enough darkness

Thunderstorm Cento

I listening pattering
slowly upstairs
to rain on the sleet roof

indoors
waves of muffled cloud
and that crackling electric smell

then through windows
the indescribable darting orange
beyond the primrose veil

and
the black thunder
of the storm's argument

sometimes
my eyes start
and I become lightning

From 'Chrysalism', The Dictionary of Obscure Sorrows, *John Koenig;
'Thunderstorm', Wikipedia;* The Go-Between, *L. P. Hartley*

SHEENA CHAPMAN

As the rain pours through winter

As the rain pours from winter
The kettle boils and erupts like a volcano
Inside with the blanket all cosy and snug
The fire lights and crackles beside the rug

The windows are having a shower
The lightning flashes in our favour
Thunder scares and warms me
Time stands still

Watching through the see-through doors
Curled up with my book from the store
Sipping my tea as I get to the chapter that ignites me
Self-care really is the best

The Irish Within

As my body is taken over by tense emotion,
unable to get rid of the work devotion,
my soul never remains still.
The vibrations that cloud my chest,
they never stop,
they never rest,
don't know if good or bad,
they are often misunderstood.

For when I take that flight,
it feels just right,
I have no kryptonite,
I remain me again.

For in the city of day drinkers,
and folk thinkers,
friendly faces and memory makers,
Dublin is like home to me.

It is more than just a place,
It's a feeling,
it's a taste,
it's an energy,
it's my soul,
for Ireland makes me whole.

Corruption

As each day unfolds
another becomes fearless and another becomes bold,
while some are clueless and rich, no real talent just a glitch,
brainwashing young minds to be like them,
while acting figured out like Barbie and Ken,
yet insecurities are what fills their chest.

Like a hollow tree that has died in the city,
for such a superficial country,
everyone thinking for other people's minds,
because people can be unkind,
are they missing the meaning of life?

Are they controlled,
or is their trauma too damn old,
looking up to Kardashians as a higher power,
this beautiful country is getting sour.

While grand canyons know the truth,
always wise, always free,
always itself its authenticity.

Roses and tulips and the winds' breeze,
is how you get out is how you feel free,
from a world with such negativity.

If you are a rose why try to be an apple,
it's a constant ongoing battle,
lakes, forests and coffee in a cup,
it's the simple things that bring me luck,
focus on the moment,
there's no need to stress,
it's only what the government wants,
it's all a test.

The Sounds that Feed my Soul

The sound of a bird's hum on a summer's day,
or tapping on the table like a drum,
high heels walking,
or people just talking,
takes my breath away,
the sheet is a piece of art,
for the whole world to see,
call me Picasso or Da Vinci,
because happiness is what great music means to be.

BIOGRAPHICAL NOTES

NATHAN ADAMS holds a BA in Aerospace Engineering with Space Technology. His first published literary works were *Felled Limbs of Trees*, *A Return to Romanticism*, and *Olivia's Sonnet*. He is most influenced by the works of Gerard Manley Hopkins, John Keats, and Pablo Neruda.

DAVID BIRKETT lives in Hitchin, where he cultivates his passions for his wife, bicycle and his cat, roughly in that order.

ADRIAN BODDY is of Irish descent and is a native of North Yorkshire. Instinctively he sides with exiles and outsiders. His first poems were written in 1969 while he was in a monastery. Now he writes every day. He also plays the violin and teaches mathematics.

LISA CHAPMAN recently moved from Letchworth to Preston, loves gardening, knitting, reading and writing poetry. Can easily be mistaken for a much older woman on paper but is actually 30! Currently studying to become a counsellor and has her own little business – making handmade healing jewellery – check it out! www.etsy.com/shop/crystalsbylis

SHEENA CHAPMAN is an aspiring musician, currently writing her own songs. You can find her in her room teaching herself to play the piano and guitar. Poetry helps with her songwriting, and she loves a good cup of tea and a social with everyone at PoetryID.

ALAN DOGGETT lives in Hitchin with his wife Lesley. His working life was split between insurance and co-owning a local fish and chip shop. He started writing in May 2020 and has published two books and also co-produced a musical.

SIMON COCKLE is a poet from Aston, Hertfordshire. His first collection is *River Lane* (Arenig Press, 2018). His poems have also appeared in *Envoi*, *iOTA*, *Dreamcatcher*, *The Lampeter Review* and *Prole Poetry*. He has read his poetry at the Ledbury Poetry Festival, in 2016, 2017 and 2019.

PAUL GREEN'S poetry includes *The Gestaltbunker* (Shearsman Books 2012), and *Shadow Times* (QBS Publications 2019). He's written speculative fiction novels – *The Qliphoth, Beneath the Pleasure Zones I & II* and *Dream Clips of the Archons,* while his radio plays have been broadcast by the BBC, CBC Canada and RTE Eire. More at paulgreenwriter.co.uk

STUART HADEN has lived in Scotland, England, Tanganyika, the USA, Anguilla and Colombia. He studied at the Architectural Association School of Architecture and has taught at the Mackintosh School of Architecture in Glasgow and the University of Texas at Austin. He now lives in Caversfield, Oxfordshire.

BARRIE KEMP has lived in 'The South' for 44 years, but his heart is still in the Midlands. Much of his literary output remains unfinished and unpublished. He is a member of Luton Poetry Society ('James Henry'), U3A and Wardown Poets. His current interests include learning the German language, books and bookshops, music and long-distance walking. He is a stout defender of public libraries and a professional educator.

DANNY LOMAS, former royal marine has an exciting past and enjoys expressing experiences in his poetry. As a tall, tattooed, muscly Northerner, Danny surprises people with his gentle nature and emotional words. His latest venture is his very own handmade soap company – www.soaptribe.co.uk

ALASTAIR McCALLION. Expat Scot living in Baldock; retired. Trying to write poetry and to relearn his mother tongue.

YUKO MINAMIKAWA ADAMS was born and grew up in Japan, and now lives in Royston. She writes poetry in Japanese and English. Her most recent collection in Japanese is Skirt. Her visual poetry works have been exhibited in Paris.

MARK RANDLES grew up in Hatfield and lives in Potters Bar. His poems have been published in several anthologies in recent years. He works for Hertfordshire Libraries as Business Improvement Manager and is married with three children and three grandchildren.

ROSE SALIBA has been writing poetry for many years and has had poems published in several anthologies. She is the author of *Simple Solutions to Stress*, published by Lapis Books. A lover of reading, writing, dancing and looking at the moon, she currently lives in Hitchin. You can find her out walking on the Common, or via: facebook.com/simplesolutionstostress

JANETTE SIBLEY, lives north of Letchworth and writes occasional prose poems. A keen walker and walk leader, Janette also sings with choirs, enjoys embroidery, Linocutting and photography.

J. JOHNSON SMITH borrows his writing name from his great-grandfather. He previously worked for Longman and other publishers. Currently he lives near Letchworth and writes for his *poetryparc* blog. He is a Poetry Society member as well as contributor to Poetry ID.

TIM TAYLOR lives in Meltham, West Yorkshire, but is a frequent visitor to Letchworth. His poems have appeared in various magazines (e.g. *Acumen, Orbis, Pennine Platform*) and anthologies. His first collection, *Sea Without a Shore*, was published in 2019 and his second, *LifeTimes*, in 2022, both by Maytree Press; he has also published two novels. For more information: https://timwordsblog.wordpress.com

ANNE TILBY makes pictures and writes poems, both humorous and serious. Her kidults do not wish to read or hear her poems, so she writes them, especially for herself. For the curious – Tilby's websites are www.bigfrieze.com and www.tilbysboatyard.com

DENNIS TOMLINSON is a retired postman, now living in London. His poems have appeared in many magazines and anthologies. His first poetry pamphlet was *Sleepless Nights* (Maverick Mustang, 2019), followed by *Over the Road* (Dempsey & Windle, 2021) and *Ornaments* (Paekakariki Press, 2022). He also served as co-editor of *Hans Sahl in Translation* (Independent Publishing Network, 2023).

DAVID VAN-CAUTER is a personal tutor and editor based in Hitchin. Arenig published his pamphlet *Mirror Lake* in 2019 and he was runner-up in the Ver Poets Open (2019) and the Bradford on Avon Prize (2017).

BARBARA WHEELER was born in London and educated in Berkshire. A retired French teacher, she lives in Hitchin with her husband and her brindled greyhound, Bertie. She aims to create word pictures capturing memorable episodes of her life and in the lives of those she loves.

JONATHAN WONHAM has lived in Hitchin since 2017. His books include *Poetry Introduction 7* (Faber and Faber, 1990), *Steel Horizon* (Incline Press, 2013), *Ordinary Others* (Drizzle-Dazzle, 2020), *Vulgar Variants* (Drizzle-Dazzle, 2021) and three volumes of *Poems for Ukraine*: *The Lady on the Plank, Until Independence Day* (both Drizzle-Dazzle, 2022) and *Without You!* (Drizzle-Dazzle, 2023). More information and poems at: www.facebook.com/JonathanWonhamPoet

ACKNOWLEDGEMENTS

J. JOHNSON SMITH

'In the Body': Highly commended, 2024 King Lear Prize.
'Corpus' was first published in *poetryparc.*

TIM TAYLOR

'I walked across a line' was first published in *Borderlands.*
'War Walk' was first published in *poetryparc.*
'Ariadne' was first published in *Ink, Sweat & Tears.*

DAVID VAN-CAUTER

'The Rules': Commended in the Waltham Forest Open competition, 2023.
'The Poetry of Climbing' was published by East Anglia Bylines for World
  Poetry Day 2024.